INTRODUCTION

A tornado is a violent, rotating wind that can occur virtually anywhere in the country. Tornadoes have been reported throughout North America, although they are most common in the Plains States. Some tornadoes develop from severe thunderstorms along or ahead of cold fronts; often these thunderstorms also produce large hail and damaging wind. Other tornadoes can arise from tropical storms and will occur just ahead of hurricanes as they make landfall.

Of the more than 1,000 tornadoes reported annually, only a small percentage is responsible for most of the damage. Those very destructive tornadoes can have winds exceeding 250 miles per hour and may carve paths more than a mile wide and up to 50 miles long.

Tornadoes can happen virtually any time of year if the conditions are right, but in general, they are most likely to occur during spring and summer months in the afternoon and early evening (between 3:00 p.m. and 9:00 p.m.).

Preparation is Key

1. Know the Dangers
Tornadoes usually occur in predictable patterns around the country on both a seasonal and geographic basis. If you are new to the area or just developing your survival awareness, learn about the tornado potential in your area. Contact your state emergency management office or local American Red Cross to learn more.

2. Learn Basic Survival Skills
Tornadoes have predictable effects; typically structures are damaged, power is knocked out, which, in turn, causes water and heating/cooling systems to fail. As a result, people can be without drinkable water, light, heat or air conditioning for days. The lack of post-disaster survival know-how creates terrible suffering and costs hundreds of lives each year.

3. Don't Panic
Staying calm is the most important thing you can do in dealing with a tornado. Excitement and alarm are natural emotions, but you must be able to manage them in order to make good decisions. Compose yourself and others and take charge of the situation.

4. Have an Action Plan
Personal safety, shelter and security are always your highest priority. Your first concern is to avoid injuries and stay safe until conditions return to normal.

- Determine the safest place to endure a tornado at home and away.
- Prepare personal survival kits for every individual in your household, including pets.
- Have a plan to connect with friends and family during and after the event so you can ensure everyone stays safe.

Waterford Press produces reference guides that introduce novices to nature, science, travel and languages. Product information and hundreds of educational games are featured on the website: www.waterfordpress.com

Scan for more info

Made in

Text and illustrations copyright © 2015 by Waterford Press Inc. All rights reserved. Images copyright © 2015 Shutterstock. Map copyright © 2006 FEMA.

To order, call 800-434-2555. For permissions, or to share comments, e-mail editor@waterfordpress.com. For information on custom-published products, call 800-434-2555 or e-mail info@waterfordpress.com.

ISBN 978-1-58355-863-8 $7.95 U.S.
50795
9 781583 558638
UPC 8 84682 01225 0

TORNADO SURVIVAL – PREPARE FOR & SURVIVE A TORNADO

A DISASTER SURVIVAL GUIDE

TORNADO SURVIVAL

PREPARE FOR & SURVIVE A TORNADO

T0123926

BEFORE – HOW TO PREPARE

Tornado Activity in the United States (1950-2006)

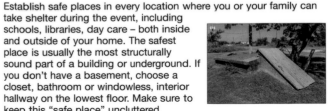

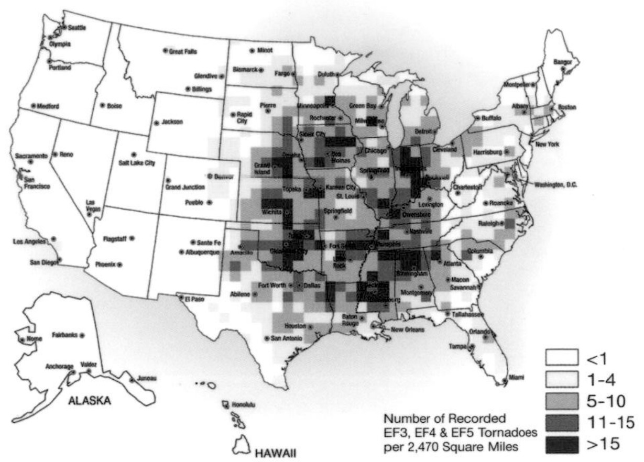
ALASKA
HAWAII
<1
1-4
5-10
11-15
>15
Number of Recorded EF3, EF4 & EF5 Tornadoes per 2,470 Square Miles

Prepare to Survive a Tornado

If you live in tornado-prone areas, take steps to ensure your family and property are as protected as possible:

- Build or reinforce a safe room. The most effective types are purpose-built underground shelters.
- With enough warning, always plan to go to a designated community shelter if you don't have your own.
- If you are at home and forced to shelter in place, know where to go and rehearse family response regularly so reactions are automatic.
- Keep a set of your essential documents away from your home – either in a bank safety deposit box or another location outside of the tornado zone so you can retrieve them should your home be destroyed.
- Stay alert for high winds.
- Keep trees trimmed and yards free of loose items and debris that can become projectiles. Consider installing storm shutters over windows and reinforcing doors.

Know the Signs of a Tornado

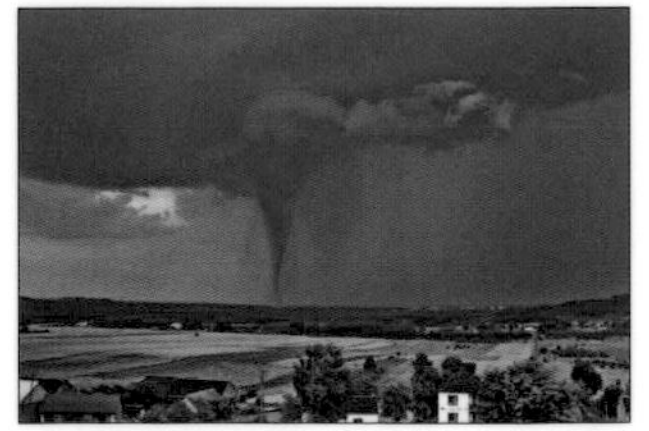

A tornado appears as a rotating, funnel-shaped cloud that extends from a thunderstorm to the ground with whirling winds. A dark, often greenish sky indicates potential hail and other tornado conditions.

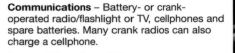

Before a tornado hits, the wind may die down and the air may become very still. A cloud of debris can mark the location of a tornado even if a funnel is not visible. Tornadoes generally occur near the trailing edge of a thunderstorm. It is not uncommon to see clear, sunlit skies behind a tornado.

- **Large hail** indicates a powerful thunderstorm. Most powerful tornadoes emerge from hail-producing thunderstorms.
- **A funnel cloud**, the visible rotating base of the cloud is a sign that a tornado may be developing.
- **A cloud of debris** can mark the path of a tornado, even if the funnel is not visible.
- **Roaring noise** – people compare the sound of an approaching tornado to that of a freight train.

BEFORE – WHAT TO EXPECT

System Failures

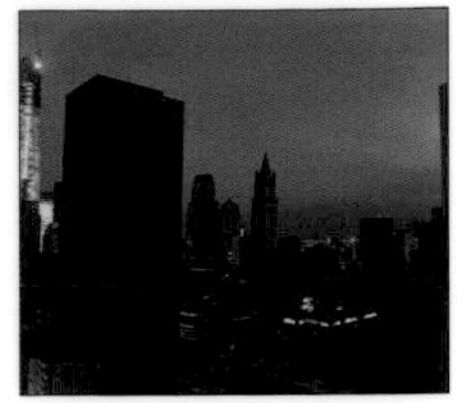

Power Failure
Electricity cut off. Downed power lines present risk of electrocution, especially if the lines are downed in water. They may also hinder your ability to leave the area. It may take days or weeks for power to return.

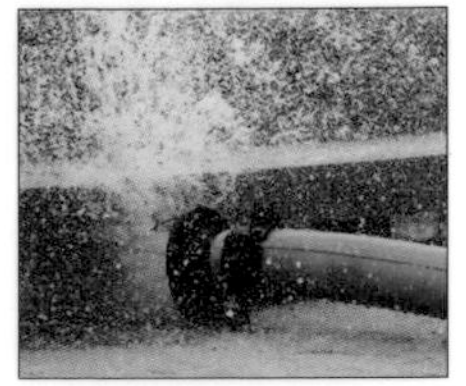

Water Failure
Water lines become damaged, water pressure fails and running water ceases. Toilets become unusable. If water lines are damaged, the water supply becomes contaminated. When water pressure returns, the water is undrinkable.

Gas Failure
Gas lines rupture and gas system fails. If gas lines are damaged, leaks present risk of poisoning, explosions and fires. Once shut off, only gas companies can restore service, which may take weeks.

Personal Risks

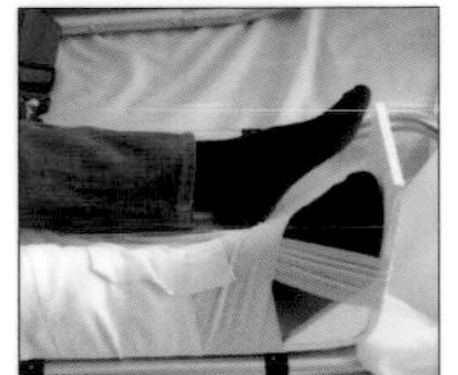

Injury
Flying or falling objects can cause deep cuts, broken bones and potentially entrap people. Trauma of events can induce heart attack.

Looting/Theft
People who are unprepared may panic and steal possessions from stores, households and individuals to survive. Have some form of defense – pepper spray or a weapon – to protect you and your family from harm.

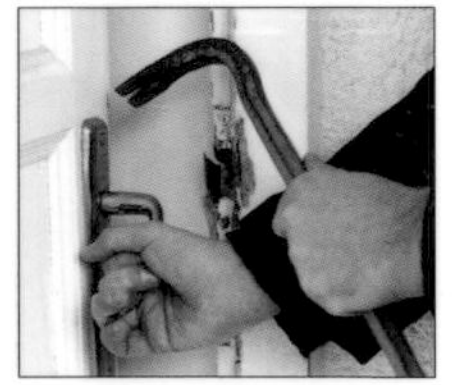

Isolation/Restricted Movement
Tornadoes commonly damage structures and uproot trees, blocking roads and bridges, which strand people where they are at the time of the event. Structural damage to homes will either trap people inside or prevent access to their homes afterward.

Tornado Alerts

The National Weather Service will use specific warnings depending on the conditions and likelihood of certain types of hazardous weather.

Scan for more info

National Weather Service

Because tornadoes cannot be "seen" well in advance, you will most often hear of a **"Hazardous Weather Watch"** as a precursor to anything more specific. This **Watch** may indicate severe thunderstorms are expected in the next few hours in a specific region. When atmospheric conditions are favorable to produce tornadoes, you will hear alerts for a **Tornado Watch.**

A **Tornado Warning** means that the event is actually happening and that your life and property are in potential danger. When a **Warning** is issued, you should take immediate action to seek shelter indoors and ideally in a basement or storm shelter.

BEFORE – CREATE AN ACTION PLAN

What to Do Before a Tornado Strikes

- If you have any warning, fill bathtubs and all available containers with water.
- Be prepared to gather your survival kit and move to 'safe room' on a moment's notice.

1. Determine the Safest Place to Endure the Event

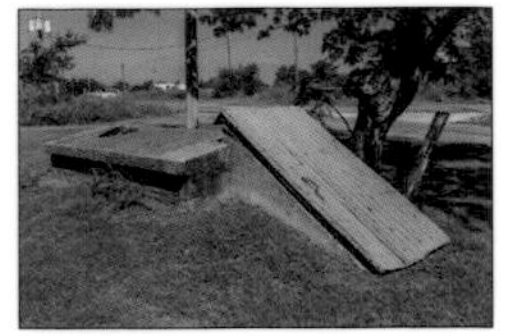

Establish safe places in every location where you or your family can take shelter during the event, including schools, libraries, day care – both inside and outside of your home. The safest place is usually the most structurally sound part of a building or underground. If you don't have a basement, choose a closet, bathroom or windowless, interior hallway on the lowest floor. Make sure to keep this "safe place" uncluttered.

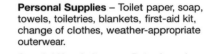

2. Know Your Local Support Network & Evacuation Routes

When a tornado strikes, survival can depend on a few basic elements. Access to clean water, shelter, warmth/cool and sanitation can be a matter of life or death in the days and weeks after a disaster event.

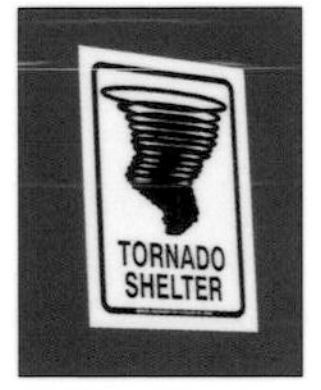
TORNADO
SHELTER

- Where are public shelters and evacuation routes, should you be required to move from your home? Learn community evacuation routes and how to get to safety. Determine where you would go and how you would get there if you needed to evacuate.
- If you have special needs such as elderly, disabled or chronically ill members in your family, what will they need and where will they go in case of disaster? Make similar arrangements for your pets.
- What are the disaster plans in places you routinely spend time, such as your workplace, your children's daycare or schools?

3. Make a Family Action Plan

- Create a card of key contacts for each family member. Have a designated contact out of the immediate area. While local phone systems may be overloaded, you can often get through to an out-of-area contact.
- Pick two places where your family can reunite after the tornado if you are apart when it strikes. One location can be your home and the other a landmark that is easy to access.

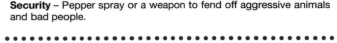

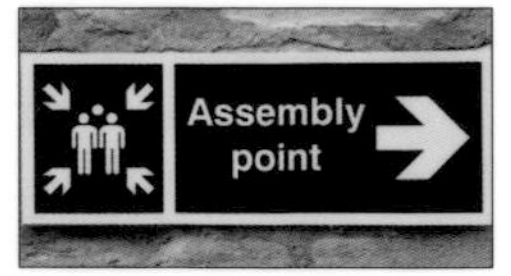
Assembly
point

- Let relatives or friends know the location of your safe room/area so they will know where to find you if you are trapped and/or injured.

4. Practice Tornado Response

Practice retreating to 'safe' areas with your family members at least twice a year. When a tornado hits, the family response should be immediate and automatic. Find and rehearse steps to get to your safe places from various locations. Learn emergency first aid and CPR to be able to help yourself and others if needed.

BEFORE – PREPARE SURVIVAL KITS

5. Prepare a Personal Survival Kit for Each Individual

Each kit should sustain an individual for three days. Put the following in a waterproof plastic container and place in an easily accessible location. Have a similar mini-kit in each vehicle.

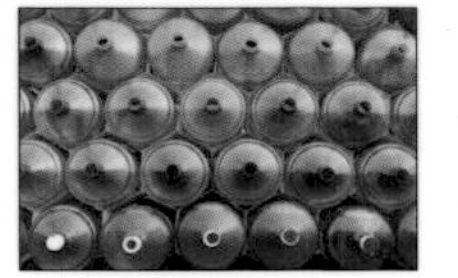

Water & Food – Three gallons of drinking water and water purification tablets. Food is not essential since you can live for weeks without eating. If you choose to include foods, they should be low in salt and high in calories and require no refrigeration or preparation (e.g., peanut butter, canned or dry food items). Replace water and food in kit every six months.

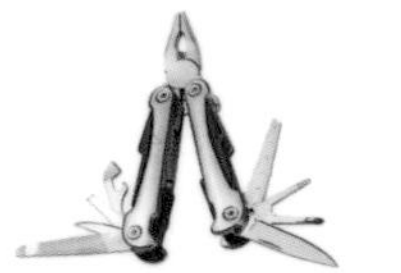

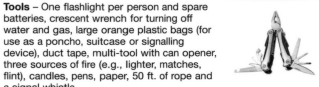

Tools – One flashlight per person and spare batteries, crescent wrench for turning off water and gas, large orange plastic bags (for use as a poncho, suitcase or signalling device), duct tape, multi-tool with can opener, three sources of fire (e.g., lighter, matches, flint), candles, pens, paper, 50 ft. of rope and a signal whistle.

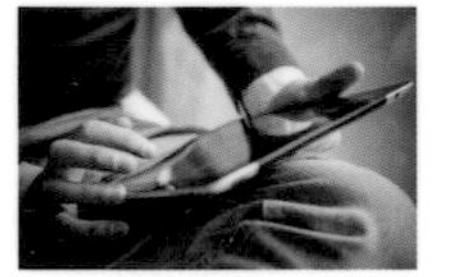

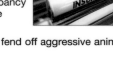

Communications – Battery- or crank-operated radio/flashlight or TV, cellphones and spare batteries. Many crank radios can also charge a cellphone.

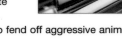

Personal Supplies – Toilet paper, soap, towels, toiletries, blankets, first-aid kit, change of clothes, weather-appropriate outerwear.

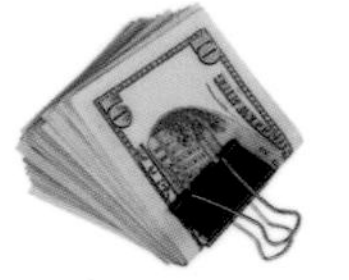

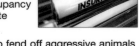

Special Needs Items – Baby formula, diapers, **medications and specialized medical equipment**, glasses, pet food, etc.

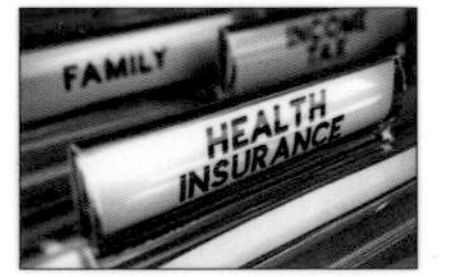
FAMILY
HEALTH
INSURANCE

Paperwork – Identification (carry with you at all times). Contact info for family, friends and emergency services, cash (small bills) and credit cards, copies of insurance papers, mortgage, bank accounts, proof of occupancy (utility bill). Keep paperwork in a separate waterproof container.

Security – Pepper spray or a weapon to fend off aggressive animals and bad people.

Survival Bucket Strategy

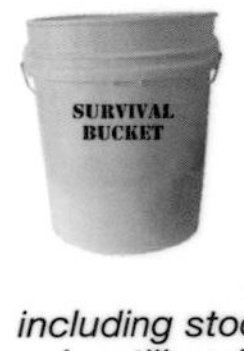
SURVIVAL
BUCKET

A simple way to prepare for disasters is to use the survival bucket strategy. Simply put, every member of a household – including pets – should have a sturdy five gallon bucket with a lid that contains enough supplies for them to survive 3 DAYS without water or power. Fill it with your survival gear (excluding phones, medications and paperwork), seal it, label it and store it where it is easy to find. Add the missing items at the last minute. A bucket is the ideal storage device because it is waterproof and also has many additional uses including stool/table, flotation device, wash basin, solar still, noisemaker for signal, water heater, bailing tool, toilet and shovel.

Scan this code to purchase survival bucket supplies online.

When a tornado approaches, **TAKE COVER IMMEDIATELY!** Get out of vehicles and stay off the roads. Most injuries during tornadoes are caused by flying glass and debris, so you need to take refuge in a sheltered area away from winds. Close all doors and windows on the side of the building facing the oncoming wind to prevent it from blowing in and lifting the roof off. If you have time, put on shoes, long pants and jackets – this may be all you have left after the event.

IF YOU ARE INDOORS

• Grab your survival kit and go to your safe room. If you are not at home, go to the lowest level of a sturdy building. Avoid places with wide-span rooftops, such as gymnasiums, stadiums, large malls, etc. These types of roofs are often damaged and offer less protection than other types of buildings. Go to the center of the building and take shelter in an interior room (closet, interior hallway) away from corners, windows, doors, glass objects and outside walls. Put as many walls as possible between you and the outside.

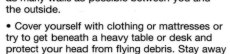
If no protection is available, protect your head with your arms and crouch.

• Cover yourself with clothing or mattresses or try to get beneath a heavy table or desk and protect your head from flying debris. Stay away from electrical equipment including phones and avoid low-lying areas that may flood.

• In a high-rise building, go to a central room away from windows or hunker down in a stairwell at the lowest level possible. Winds will be strongest on the upper floors.

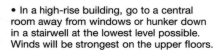

• Do not open windows.

IF YOU ARE IN A TRAILER OR MOBILE HOME

• Get out immediately and go to the lowest floor of a sturdy, nearby building or a storm shelter. Mobile homes, even if tied down, offer little protection from tornadoes.

IF YOU ARE OUTDOORS

• Try to find a place lower than ground level, like a ditch, where you will be less likely to be hit by flying debris. Cover your head with your hands. Do not take refuge under an overpass or bridge.

IF YOU ARE IN A VEHICLE

• Try to drive to the closest sturdy shelter. If your vehicle is hit by flying debris while you are driving, pull over and leave the vehicle immediately for safe shelter.

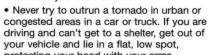

• Never try to outrun a tornado in urban or congested areas in a car or truck. If you are driving and can't get to a shelter, get out of your vehicle and lie in a flat, low spot, protecting your head with your arms.

• Avoid highway overpasses and bridges as they can be damaged by flying debris and may collapse on you.

---

1. Is Your Location Still Safe and Secure?

If you see anything that is unsafe, take your survival kit and get everyone out of the building immediately. Damaged structures can entrap or injure people when they collapse.

• Look for damage in your immediate surroundings.

• If you smell gas, hear a hissing or blowing noise, immediately leave the building. If you can, turn off the gas at the outside main valve and call the gas company or notify emergency personnel of the damage.

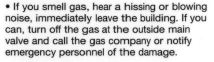

• If you see frayed wiring or sparks, or if there is an odor of something burning, leave the building unless you are able to shut off the electrical system at the main circuit breaker.

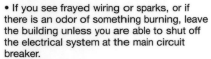

• If your location is not safe and secure and has become damaged, go to a designated public shelter. **Text SHELTER + your ZIP code to 4FEMA** to find the nearest shelter in your area.

• If you are trapped, do not light a match. Create a signal to draw attention to your location. Tap on a pipe or wall so rescuers can locate you. Use a whistle if one is available. Shout only as a last resort. Shouting can cause you to inhale dangerous amounts of dust.

Scan for more info

FEMA

2. Is Anyone Injured or Trapped?

Help injured or trapped persons. Check on neighbors who may require special assistance with infants, the elderly and people with accessibility and medical/functional needs.

• Assess and treat any minor injuries as you are qualified and able to do so. Stop a bleeding injury by applying direct pressure to the wound. When bleeding stops, apply a dry sterile dressing. Have any serious injuries evaluated by a physician as soon as possible.

• Do not attempt to move seriously injured people unless they are in immediate danger of further injury. Get medical assistance immediately. If someone has stopped breathing, begin CPR.

3. Making Contact With Others

Contact all family members and friends to assure they do not need assistance. If you or a member of your family become separated or goes missing, DO NOT CALL THE POLICE; they will be overwhelmed with other demands. Instead, contact the American Red Cross at 1-800-RED-CROSS/1-800-733-2767.

Scan for more info

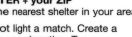

Red Cross

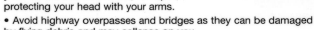
• On average, about 60 people are killed by tornadoes every year.
• Trauma injuries from flying or falling debris are the most frequent cause of death.

---

4. Moving Around After a Tornado

As you prepare to move, remember that personal safety, shelter and security are always your highest priority. Moving can expose you to potential injuries and create further problems if you are not careful. Protect yourself from further injury by putting on appropriate clothes – shirts, long pants, boots and gloves if they are available.

Most injuries occur after the tornado has passed, when people are trying to rescue others or clean up debris. Nails, broken glass and collapsing structures are the visible hazards; downed electrical wires, gas leaks and contaminated water are harder to see, but deadly.

General Safety Considerations

• Continue to monitor your cellphone, radio or television for emergency information.

• If you are away from home, do not return until authorities say it is safe to do so.

• Be careful when moving through structures that have been damaged.

• Check for leaking gas and water. If you suspect any damage to your home, shut off electrical power, natural gas and propane tanks to avoid fire, electrocution or explosions.

• Use battery-powered lanterns or headlamps rather than gas-powered lamps or candles for light sources when the power is out.

• If there has been significant water damage, do not turn on the power until an electrician has checked the wiring to ensure it's safe. It is easy to electrocute yourself when things are damp, even when changing a fuse.

• Do not go near downed power lines or objects in contact with downed lines. If water is in the vicinity of downed lines, the whole area may be electrified. Report electrical hazards to the police and the utility company.

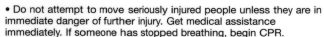

• Open cabinets cautiously. Beware of objects that can fall off shelves.

• Clean up spilled medicines, drugs, flammable liquids and other potentially hazardous materials that could become a fire hazard.

• Do not use tap water unless you are certain it is safe; cracks in pipes can cause inadvertent flooding and risk of contamination.

UNSEEN HAZARDS
• Carbon monoxide
• Contaminated water
• Electrocution
• Falling objects

• Check your heating ducts for blockages; blocked systems can cause a buildup of carbon monoxide. If you have any doubts, have an expert inspect the system before turning it on.

• For insurance purposes, take pictures of any damages.

Survival Priorities

Statistically speaking, the most likely causes of death during a disaster are becoming too cold (hypothermia) or too hot (hyperthermia). Depending on where you live – Anchorage vs. Phoenix – your survival strategy and the contents of your survival kit should be adapted to suit your environment.

Shelter

Protection from the elements will allow you to preserve strength and restore energy. If your safe area becomes compromised during the storm, either repair the damages or move to another shelter.

In Cold Weather

1. Insulate an area suitable for the number of people in your group. Close large openings with duct tape and tarps, plastic, cardboard or blankets, depending on what is available to you. **BE CAREFUL** to leave adequate airflow or you will suffocate!

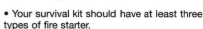

2. Protect yourself from loss of body warmth by adding layers of dry materials – cardboard, rugs, blankets, cushions, clothing or mattresses – between you and the floor or earth.

3. Stay as dry as possible.

In Warm Weather

1. Stay as hydrated as possible; limit exertion.

2. Protect yourself from the elements; stay out of the sun and wind, which deplete hydration.

3. Stay on the lowest floor of your house, where it is coolest. If outdoors, seek the safest source of shade and build your shelter around/under that. If there is ample fresh water available, wet your clothes to increase cooling.

Water

You can only survive 3 days without water, and even less in hot, arid surroundings. Carefully ration the fresh water you have for drinking only (one gallon per person per day under normal conditions). Never waste water; after use for cooking and bathing, it can be used as gray water for other purposes.

Drinking Water

Can be obtained from several sources. In addition to the water stored in tub(s) and sinks, sources of fresh water inside a building include:

Water pipes – Once you shut off the water to a building, the water pipes remain full of water. Turn off your hot water heater and water treatment system and drain the water from the pipes via taps into food-quality containers.

Hot water heater – The hot water heater in most homes contains 20-30 gallons of water. Simply drain from the faucet at the bottom.

Toilet tanks – Each holds 2-4 gallons. Purify before drinking.

Hot water heater

Gray Water

Use gray water from streams, ponds, puddles and snowmelt for uses other than drinking. Most gray water can be purified for drinking if needed.

To flush a toilet, fill a bucket with one gallon of gray water. Pour the water into the toilet bowl in one thrust, fast enough to push the contents of the bowl down the drain. If the sewage system is damaged, do not flush toilets or drain sinks as it may trigger a "backwash" that would further damage your home.

How to Purify Water

If the water system fails, NEVER drink tap water unless you are certain it is not contaminated. To be safe, water should always be purified before drinking.

Three simple ways to purify water are:

1. Bring water to a rolling boil for 10 minutes;

2. Treat with purification tablets, iodine (12 drops per gallon) or bleach (1/2 tablespoon per gallon);

3. Use a water pump or gravity-fed purifier to strain bacteria from the water.

Fire

With fire/heat you can purify water, control your core temperature, cook or preserve food and signal for rescue.

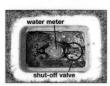

• Your survival kit should have at least three types of fire starter.

• Your barbecue, camping stove or gas lanterns are a potential source of heat that can be used to heat and purify water, warm and cook foods. Never use indoors; carbon monoxide released from these burning gases will kill you.

• Portable generators can provide temporary power to key sources like the refrigerator and heating/cooling system. Ensure you have enough gas to keep it running sporadically for several days.

The Silent Killer

Never use generators, grills, camp stoves or other gasoline, propane, natural gas or charcoal-burning devices inside your home, garage or camper. Carbon monoxide (CO) – an odorless, colorless gas that is given off when these fuels are burned – can cause sudden illness and death if you breathe it. If you suspect CO poisoning and are feeling dizzy, light-headed or nauseated, get into fresh air and seek medical help immediately. Even burning candles in an airtight room can cause asphyxiation and death.

Locate the main shutoff valves to your home or building before you are faced with an emergency. **Listen carefully to news reports that will inform you when to turn off your utilities.**

Power

Shut off electricity to the house to avoid power surges that can cause fires. Locate the power breaker box. If you have circuit breakers, there is usually a double breaker at the top of the row of breakers marked 'Main'. Flip that one and it shuts the house power off. Otherwise, simply turn off each individual breaker. Disconnect electrical appliances.

Water

To turn off the water to the building, locate the main shut-off valve (usually under a metal plate near the street at the front of the building). Lift off the plate and use a crescent wrench to turn the valve clockwise about 1/4 of a turn to shut the water off. In many homes, a secondary shut-off valve is located in the garage or basement. If the building is on a well, find out where the shut-off valve is.

water meter
shut-off valve

Gas

Gas lines can rupture, causing gas flow to fail. Leaking gas presents risks of poisoning, explosions and fires. Locate your gas meter outside the building. The shutoff valve is attached to the pipe coming out of the ground. Use a crescent wrench to turn the valve clockwise about 1/4 of a turn to shut off the gas. **Once the gas is turned off, you need a professional to turn it back on, which could take weeks.**

Crescent Wrench

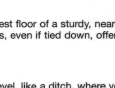

shut-off valve

Emergency Etiquette

• Cooperate fully with public safety officials. If asked to relocate, do so immediately. Failure to relocate when asked creates an unfair load on emergency response personnel to find or rescue you, instead of on the community-wide recovery operations that will help everyone get back home as quickly and safely as possible.

• Only use your telephone for urgent calls to avoid tying up the available airspace.

• Keep your children and animals under your direct control.

• Report failures in power, water and gas to local utilities.

• Respond to requests for volunteer assistance by police, fire fighters and relief organizations, but **do not go into damaged areas unless assistance has been requested.**

• If you are going to a community shelter, bring your emergency supplies. Your stay will be more comfortable if you have your own food, water, clothes, blankets/sleeping bags and some activities (books, cards, etc.) with which to pass the time. Access to power sources will be limited, so take extra batteries for your communications devices.